AF269444

ITALY

R.L. Van

Big Buddy Books
An Imprint of Abdo Publishing
abdobooks.com

abdobooks.com

Published by Abdo Publishing, a division of ABDO, PO Box 398166, Minneapolis, Minnesota 55439. Copyright © 2023 by Abdo Consulting Group, Inc. International copyrights reserved in all countries. No part of this book may be reproduced in any form without written permission from the publisher. Big Buddy Books™ is a trademark and logo of Abdo Publishing.

Printed in the United States of America, North Mankato, Minnesota
102022
012023

Design: Emily O'Malley, Mighty Media, Inc.
Production: Mighty Media, Inc.
Editor: Jessica Rusick
Cover Photograph: muratart/Shutterstock Images
Interior Photographs: Alessandro Tortora/Shutterstock Images, p. 6 (bottom); Andrea Raffin/Shutterstock Images, p. 23; Apostolis Giontzis/Shutterstock Images, p. 9; Asatur Yesayants/Shutterstock Images, p. 21; Creative Travel Projects/Shutterstock Images, p. 15; elvirkins/Shutterstock Images, p. 19; Everett Collection/Shutterstock Images, p. 29 (top left); Filip Bjorkman/Shutterstock Images, p. 7 (map); IR Stone/Shutterstock Images, p. 11; Jerome PARIS/Shutterstock Images, p. 27 (top right); Julia Zavalishina/Shutterstock Images, p. 6 (middle); Lapadus Daniel/Shutterstock Images, p. 28 (bottom); lukulo/iStockphoto, pp. 5 (compass), 7 (compass); Maryna Pleshkun/Shutterstock Images, p. 30 (currency); Media Home/Shutterstock Images, p. 30 (flag); muratart/Shutterstock Images, p. 26 (left); NickolayV/Shutterstock Images, p. 28 (top); Philipp Dase/Shutterstock Images, p. 13; posztos/Shutterstock Images, p. 27 (top left); Pyty/Shutterstock Images, p. 5 (map); Rhys Leis/Shutterstock Images, p. 26 (right); S-F/Shutterstock Images, p. 25; Stefano Buttafoc/Shutterstock Images, p. 17; V_E/Shutterstock Images, p. 29 (bottom); Viacheslav Lopatin/Shutterstock Images, p. 27 (bottom); Vladimir Sazonov/Shutterstock Images, p. 6 (top); Wikimedia Commons, p. 29 (top right)
Design Elements: Mighty Media, Inc.
Country population and area figures taken from the CIA World Factbook

Library of Congress Control Number: 2022940510

Publisher's Cataloging-in-Publication Data
Names: Van, R.L., author.
Title: Italy / by R.L. Van
Description: Minneapolis, Minnesota : Abdo Publishing, 2023 | Series: Countries | Includes online resources and index.
Identifiers: ISBN 9781532199660 (lib. bdg.) | ISBN 9781098274863 (ebook)
Subjects: LCSH: Italy--Juvenile literature. | Europe--Juvenile literature. | Italy--History--Juvenile literature. | Geography--Juvenile literature.
Classification: DDC 945--dc23

CONTENTS

PASSPORT TO ITALY

Italy is a country in southern Europe. More than 61 million people live there. It is on the Mediterranean Sea. It has many islands.

WHERE IS ITALY?
N
W E
S
Austria
Switzerland
Slovenia
France
San Marino
ITALY
Corsica
Vatican City
Sardinia
Mediterranean Sea
Sicily

IMPORTANT CITIES

Rome is Italy's **capital** and largest city. It is known for its history, historic ruins, and art.

Milan is Italy's second-largest city. It is known as a center of business, fashion, and culture.

Naples is Italy's third-largest city. Pizza was invented here. The city is also known for its nearby active **volcano**, Mount Vesuvius.

Milan
Population: 3.15 million
ITALY
N
W
E
S
SAY IT
Rome
ROHM
Milan
muh-LAHN
Naples
NAY-puhlz
Rome
Population: 4.3 million
Naples
Population: 2.18 million
DID YOU KNOW?
Milan is considered one of the fashion centers of the world.

ITALY IN HISTORY

The city of Rome was founded in 753 BCE. It became the heart of the Roman **Empire**, which began in 27 BCE. The ancient Romans had a very advanced civilization.

The Roman Empire split apart in 395 CE. Afterward, different groups fought to control the land.

Ancient Romans used the Roman Forum for court, meetings, and gladiator fights.

····DID YOU····
KNOW?

At its strongest, the Roman **Empire** included more than 45 million people.

The Renaissance began in Italy in the 1300s. This was a time of learning, ideas, and art. By 1871, Italy became a country.

Around 1922, **fascist** Benito Mussolini became Italy's leader. At first, Italy fought for Germany in **World War II**. Then it fought against Germany. In 1946, Italy became a **republic**.

The Italian artist Raphael painted *School of Athens* during the Renaissance. The work shows famous thinkers.

AN IMPORTANT SYMBOL

Italy's flag has green, white, and red stripes. It was based on France's flag. But it uses the colors of Milan.

Italy is a **parliamentary republic**. The two houses of parliament make laws. The president is head of state. The prime minister is head of government.

The green on Italy's
flag stands for hope.
White stands for faith.
Red stands for charity.

13

ACROSS THE LAND

Italy has coasts, forests, rivers, islands, and **volcanoes**. The Po Valley has rich farmland. The Alps and Apennines are mountain ranges.

Wolves, wild boars, deer, and lynx live in Italy. Heather, water lilies, and many types of trees grow there.

The Dolomites are part of the Alps. This range has jagged, rocky peaks.

EARNING A LIVING

Factory workers in Italy make cars, medicines, leather, and more. Many people have service jobs in business, sales, and tourism.

Italy's farmland is its most important **natural resource**. Farmers grow grapes, olives, and grains. They raise pigs, cattle, sheep, and goats.

Italy's Tuscany region
is world-famous for
its grape vineyards.

LIFE IN ITALY

Most Italian people live in cities. Favorite Italian foods include pasta, pizza, cheese, risotto, and meat. Wine and coffee are popular drinks.

Italian people enjoy soccer, basketball, and biking. Most Italians are Roman Catholic. This religion is based in Vatican City, a country inside Rome.

Pizza Margherita is a classic
Italian dish. It has basil,
mozzarella, and tomato sauce.

FAMOUS FACES

Arianna Fontana was born in Sondrio, Italy. At age 16, she won a bronze medal for speed skating at the 2006 Winter Olympics. This made her the youngest Italian to ever win a Winter Olympics medal! By 2022, Fontana had won more Winter Olympic medals than any other Italian person.

By 2022, Arianna
Fontana had won
11 Olympic medals.

Andrea Bocelli was born in Lajatico, Italy. He is a singer known for mixing opera and pop music. Bocelli's 1997 album *Romanza* is his best-selling album to date. Bocelli is blind. In 2011, he started a foundation to help people with disabilities and people in poverty.

Andrea Bocelli (*right*) and his son Matteo performed together at Italy's *Festival di Sanremo* in 2019.

A GREAT COUNTRY

Italy has beautiful buildings and a rich history and culture. The people and places of Italy help make the world a more interesting place.

Italy has more than 400 islands! Capri is popular with tourists. It has a famous sea cave with bright blue water and ancient Roman ruins.

TOUR BOOK

If you ever visit Italy, here are some places to go and things to do!

EXPLORE

Ride in a gondola in Venice. This famous port city is actually a group of islands.

EAT

Have pizza in Naples, where it was invented!

LISTEN

See an opera at the Teatro alla Scala opera house in Milan.

LEARN

Visit the Galileo Museum in Florence to learn about the famous astronomer Galileo Galilei.

REMEMBER

Visit the ruins of Pompeii. The city was destroyed when Mount Vesuvius erupted in 79 CE.

TIMELINE

476

The western part of the Roman **Empire** broke apart. The eastern part became the Byzantine Empire.

1436

Filippo Brunelleschi's dome for the cathedral of Florence was completed. Building it was a major engineering accomplishment.

ABOUT 1296

Famous Italian explorer Marco Polo completed his famous book about his travels to Asia.

ABOUT 1503

Leonardo da Vinci began painting the *Mona Lisa*.

1796

Napoleon I of France invaded Italy for the first time.

2020

The MOSE flood barrier was finished to protect Venice from increasingly high waters.

2013

Pope Francis became the new leader of the Roman Catholic Church. He now lives in Vatican City.

ITALY
UP CLOSE

Official Name
Repubblica Italiana
(Italian Republic)

Flag

Population
61,095,551 (2022 est.)
24th-most-populated country

Total Area
116,348 square miles
(301,340 sq km)
72nd-largest country

Official Language
Italian

Capital
Rome

Currency
Euro

Form of Government
Parliamentary republic

National Anthem
"Il Canto degli
Italiani" ("The Song
of the Italians")

GLOSSARY

capital—a city where government leaders meet.

empire—a large group of states or countries under one ruler called an emperor or empress.

fascist (FASH-ist)—a person who believes in valuing nation and race above individuals. A fascist government has a ruler who controls many parts of people's lives.

natural resource—something useful or valuable from nature.

parliamentary republic—a government that has a leader who is usually a president, not a king or queen, and a parliament that makes laws.

republic—a government in which the people choose the leader.

volcano—a deep opening in Earth's surface from which hot liquid rock or steam comes out.

World War II—a war fought in Europe, Asia, and Africa from 1939 to 1945.

ONLINE RESOURCES

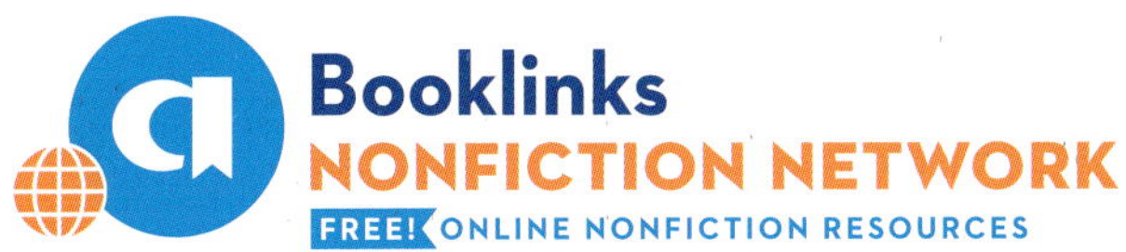

To learn more about Italy, please visit **abdobooklinks.com** or scan this QR code. These links are routinely monitored and updated to provide the most current information available.

INDEX